Ling

Krystle

Sally

Preeti

Jess

SPECIAL BROWNIE SAYING

Lend a Hand.

BROWNIE GUIDE LAW

A Brownie Guide thinks of others before herself and does a Good Turn every day.

Contents

'Take a look at what's inside your fabulous 2011 Brownie Annual!'

Be safe

You should be able to have a go at everything in your *Brownie Annual*, but sometimes it is a good idea to get some help. When you see this symbol, ask an adult if they can lend a hand.

Be safe

Badges!

Look out for this sign. If you enjoyed the activity on that page, you might like to try the badge, too!

Web safe

This symbol means you should follow your Brownie Web Safe Code. To remember it look up page 8 in your Brownie Badge Book or visit www.girlguiding.org.uk/ brownies/websafe.

Web safe

Girlguiding UK
girls in the lead

Published by Girlguiding UK
17–19 Buckingham Palace Road
London SW1W 0PT
www.girlguiding.org.uk

© The Guide Association 2010

Girlguiding UK is an operating name of The Guide Association. Registered charity number 306016. Incorporated by Royal Charter.
ISBN 978 0 85260 247 8

Girlguiding UK Trading Service ordering code 6005

All Brownie and Guide photographs © The Guide Association.

Other photographs courtesy of Shutterstock unless otherwise stated.

Book covers for 'Top ten reads' © as stated on pages 74–75.

Girlguiding UK would like to thank all the Brownies and their Leaders who took part in the development and production of this resource.

Project Editors: Mariano Kälfors, Harriet Lowe, Alice Proctor
Writers: Alison Griffiths, Emma Joyce, Mariano Kälfors, Abigail Latter, Jennifer Lockey,

Harriet Lowe, Chris Morphy-Godber, Helen Mortimer, Alice Proctor, Nithya Rae, Hannah Rainford, Anna Smirnova
Designers: Helen Davis, Angie Daniel, Kim Haddrell, Yuan Zhuang
Production: Wendy Reynolds
Project Coordinator: Helen Channa

Printed by Scotprint.

Readers are reminded that during the lifespan of this publication there may be changes to Girlguiding UK's policy, or legal requirements, that may affect the accuracy of the information contained within these pages.

Sally's style quiz

What's your style?

'Circle your answer to each question then find out where it takes you!'

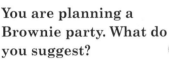

On Brownie Holiday your Leaders ask what you'd like to do next. What do you suggest?
a. You don't mind, so long as it's fun.
b. Something outside as it's sooooo sunny!
c. Something that everyone can enjoy.
d. Making up your own game.
e. Lots of different things – you are full of great ideas.

You are planning a Brownie party. What do you suggest?
a. Fun games – it's got to be a laugh!
b. Loads of action. Can it be outside?
c. Games that help Brownies get to know each other better.
d. A fancy dress party.
e. A good plan so that there's something for everyone.

Your Six wants to raise some money for a local charity. What's your idea?
a. Staging a joke and comedy show – everyone likes a laugh.
b. A sponsored swim or bike ride.
c. A special charity Lend a Hand day – it's nice helping people.
d. Creating recycled toys to sell.
e. Organising a fête – you're happy to sort it all out.

Illustrated by Andi Good

Half way through term a new girl joins Brownies. What happens next?
a. You hope she joins your Six as it's great meeting new people.
b. You talk with her to find out how much she likes sport.
c. Your Leader asks if you'll be her Brownie Buddy.
d. You wonder if she'll help you create outfits for the Unit fashion show.
e. You go straight up to her and welcome her to Brownies. You ask her all about herself.

You're outside playing your favourite game when it starts raining. How do you react?
a. Get on with making the best of being inside.
b. Wish it wasn't raining – being active is more fun than sitting around!
c. You don't mind – you're with your mates.
d. Start dreaming up the best indoor game you could play.
e. You're first inside, organising the new game so no time is wasted!

On an outdoor ramble your Leader gives you a list of things to look out for. How well do you do?
a. OK – you were so busy having a giggle you missed a few.
b. Really well. You only missed one because you were busy racing about.
c. Could do better! Less chatting with your mates next time.
d. Fairly well – you sketched quite a few so didn't have time to see them all.
e. You got them all – and photographed each one to show your Leader.

6

HAPPY-GO-LUCKY LAND

MOSTLY AS
You're laid-back and friendly. You're always positive about new ideas and like everyone to enjoy themselves.

WILD WORLD BY THE SEA

MOSTLY BS
You are energetic, adventurous and like to learn new skills. You love sporty activities – and being outdoors.

NEW PEOPLE PLANET

MOSTLY CS
You enjoy being with people, helping them and getting to know others.

CLOUD NINE

MOSTLY DS
You are creative, fun and like to daydream. You also like having fun with others.

GO-GETTER

MOSTLY ES
You like to help and are bursting with great ideas. Both organised and determined, you like things done properly!

How did you do?

LUCY ABI ASHA KATIE EMMA SB

SUPER BROWNIE AND THE BIG FREEZE

I'm so excited about our Brownie Holiday this weekend!

Yeah! I hope we can do lots outdoors.

I'm really looking forward to the zip wire!

Abseiling!

Archery!

Kayaking!

Do we really need to bring our wellies and waterproofs?

And thermals!

Yes. Better to be prepared than sorry.

But it's May!

We're in the UK. In May, anything can happen.

There's no way we'll be wearing these.

I hope not!

Illustrated by Toni Goffe

THAT WEEKEND

Are we nearly there yet?

For the thousandth time – no!

We interrupt this programme to bring you a severe weather warning. About 20cm of snow is expected across Britain later tonight with freezing temperatures.

Wow!

BROWNIES ARRIVE AT FOXLEASE TRAINING AND ACTIVITY CENTRE

We're here, Brownies.

Yaaaay!

Hello, Brownies! I'm Wendy. Welcome to Foxlease. We've got some fab activities planned for you. First, let's get you settled in Princess Margaret Lodge.

LATER THAT DAY

This is *so* cool!

This is exciting!

I'm having so much fun!

Wheeee!

Scary!

I'm exhausted.

I'm ready for bed.

Let's clear up then you can get into your jimjams.

Hey, look! It's snowing outside.

Who's that at the door?

Ace!

Hello, can you help? These Guides were meant to be camping outside tonight. They need shelter. Could they stay with you?

Yes, of course.

Thanks! I hope the snow stops soon. The coach with the rest of our unit still hasn't arrived.

They're stuck on the motorway. They could be there all night.

Oh, no!

Don't worry, I'll take care of it.

Thanks, Super Brownie!

No problem!

LATER THAT DAY

Who'd have guessed we needed our cold weather clothes!

You can never be too prepared – even in May!

It's nearly time to leave, but how will we get home with all this snow on the roads?

The motorways are fine, but the side roads haven't been cleared.

I'll take care of it!

Goodbye!

Thank you!

Goodbye, Brownies!

THE END

Jess's fun facts

Strange sports

'Football not your thing? Golf too boring? Take a look at these weird and wonderful sports!'

CABER TOSSING

This Scottish sport needs a lot of strength! A caber is a very long, heavy wooden pole not unlike a telephone pole. To start with the thrower picks up the caber, balancing it on one end. After running a few steps, the person throws the caber so it bounces on its other end. It should flip over before falling to the ground. To score maximum points the caber must topple straight over after it bounces. If it goes to the right or the left the thrower gets fewer points.

CAMEL RACING

In the Middle East, camels are raced like horses are in the UK. Jockeys have to ride their camel a certain distance and the first camel over the line wins.

In Australia, there is an annual camel-racing championship called the Camel Cup. Take a look at **www.camelcup.com.au** to see what it's all about.

Web safe

TOE WRESTLING

In Derbyshire, England, there is an annual toe-wrestling competition with both men's and ladies' championships. Competitors face each other with their heels placed either side of a wrestling board and their big toes interlocked. The wrestling board is a special board with high ends. The idea is to push the other person's foot over so it touches the end of the board. Players must keep their bottoms and hands on the floor the whole time – and their other foot off the ground!

CUP STACKING

This sport involves stacking plastic cups in a set formation as quickly as possible. This usually means making them into pyramid shapes. The race isn't over until the cups are returned to their starting shape, so finding the quickest way to dismantle the pyramid is as important as the stacking. Look at the video clips at **http://greatbritain. speedstacks.com/about/ history.php** to see how it's done.

Web safe

PARKOUR

This can be done by individuals or groups. The aim is to get from one place to another using the shortest route. Players need to find the quickest way of getting over anything that is in their way – by climbing, leap-frogging or jumping. The movements need to be graceful and look beautiful, almost like dancing.

Be safe

Don't try any of these activities at home. Talk with an adult you know before trying any new sport or activity to make sure you stay safe.

BADGE LINK
World cultures

13

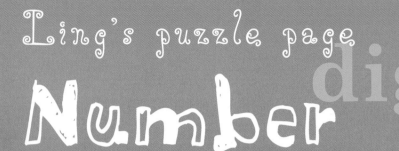

Ling's puzzle page
Number crunchers

'I know what you're thinking – numbers, fun? Yeah, right! With these great puzzles, jokes and tricks, you'll soon see that numbers aren't boring at all.'

Q. Why was six afraid of seven?
A. Because seven ate nine!

BADGE LINK

Entertainer

Number fun

MATHEMAGICS!

A great trick to amaze your friends!

1. Write the number 9 on a piece of paper. Seal it in an envelope.
2. Ask your friend to write down a three-digit number. Each digit must be different and the first highest.
3. Ask her to jumble up the digits to make a smaller number and write that below the first one.
4. Tell her to take away the smaller number from the bigger number.
5. Get her to add up the digits in the answer (then again if it's a two-digit answer at first).
6. Announce that you had already worked out her answer. Ask her to open your envelope.

The answer is always 9! Whatever number is chosen, or however many digits it has, this trick will work.

Q. Which snakes are good at maths?
A. Adders!

CROSS NUMBERS

Fill in this grid with numbers by solving the clues

Across
1. A gross
2. A baker's dozen
3. One short of a century
4. Three dozen
5. 4 × 4
6. A score
7. C – XX
9. Five centuries
10. Number of days in five weeks

Down
1. A decade is __ years
2. The year guiding began
4. 2,000 + 1,000
6. XXIV
7. 100 – 15
8. Three-quarters of a century

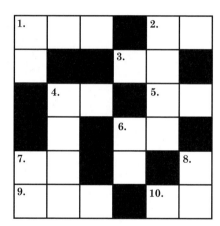

Number 12 walks into a bar and orders a pint of beer. The barman doesn't serve him. He asks, 'Why aren't you serving me?' The barman replies, 'Sorry, but you aren't 18.'

Number fact!

The figures we use to write numbers today (1, 2, 3 and so on) are called Arabic numerals. They were in fact from India and reached Europe through Iraq and North Africa about 800 years ago.

ANCIENT NUMBERS

Have you ever seen Roman numerals? Find out more and tackle some number challenges!

I is 1
II is 2 (**I** + **I**)
III is 3 (**I** + **I** + **I**)
Rather than use **IIII** for 4, the Romans wrote it as the number before 5.
5 is **V**, so 4 is **IV** (1 less than 5).
Numbers 6, 7 and 8 follow the pattern of adding 1s to 5.
VI is 6 (**V** + **I**)
VII is 7 (**V** + **II**)
VIII is 8 (**V** + **III**)
With 9, the Romans wrote it as the number before 10.
10 is **X**, so 9 is **IX**.
10 to 20 are simply 10 (**X**) plus the number 1, 2, 3 and so on, so:
12 is **XII**
14 is **XIV**
17 is **XVII**
19 is **XIX**
20 is **XX**
These letters are used for larger numbers.
L is 50
C is 100
D is 500
M is 1,000

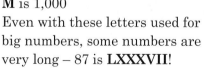

Even with these letters used for big numbers, some numbers are very long – 87 is **LXXXVII**!
Have a go at these sums.
Answers in Roman, of course!
II + **III** =
XXV + **V** =
VI – **I** =
L – **VII** =
XI + **IV** =
And, finally, what's **MMXI**?

Krystle's growing garden

Life in miniature

'Have you ever wondered what life would look like if you were the size of a ladybird? Make your own little world with this great idea.'

YOU WILL NEED

- ☆ large shallow tub or tray, like a shallow seed tray
- ☆ soil or potting compost
- ☆ small plants
- ☆ figures and other items to decorate (things that won't go mushy sitting on damp soil)

BEFORE YOU START

If you are using real plants ask an adult to help you make holes in the bottom of your tub. Sit the tub on a tray if you are going to keep it inside.

2 With your fingers, make a hole in your soil big enough for your first plant.

1 Fill your tub with soil. Make small hills and mounds so your world is more interesting.

3 Gently take the plant out of its pot. Don't pull it by the stem but squeeze round the outside of the pot to loosen it.

4 Put your plant in the hole. Press the soil around it so that it stands firm.

5 Once all your plants are in place you can add paths that wind round them.

BADGE LINK

Gardener
Toymaker
Craft
Designer

PLANTS YOU COULD USE

☆ Tiny cacti – mind your fingers!

☆ Pansies, busy lizzies and other bedding plants.

☆ Ivy with small leaves (Kenilworth ivy).

☆ Moss.

☆ Baby's tears (this is a great plant with tiny leaves).

☆ Alpines.

DECORATIONS

☆ Toy cars.

☆ Gravel or sand to mark out paths.

☆ Shells, beads and ribbons.

☆ Stones and rocks – paint them with acrylic paint.

☆ A shallow dish covered in foil makes a great pond.

☆ Twigs, straws, lolly sticks or cocktail sticks for fences, flags, banners or road signs.

☆ Lego™ or other building blocks to make a house.

☆ Salt dough figures painted with acrylic paints – use the dough recipe on pages 26–27.

6 Now add figures, cars, signs and anything else to liven up your world.

Make sure your plants get plenty of light and water them regularly.

Preeti's fill-in fun

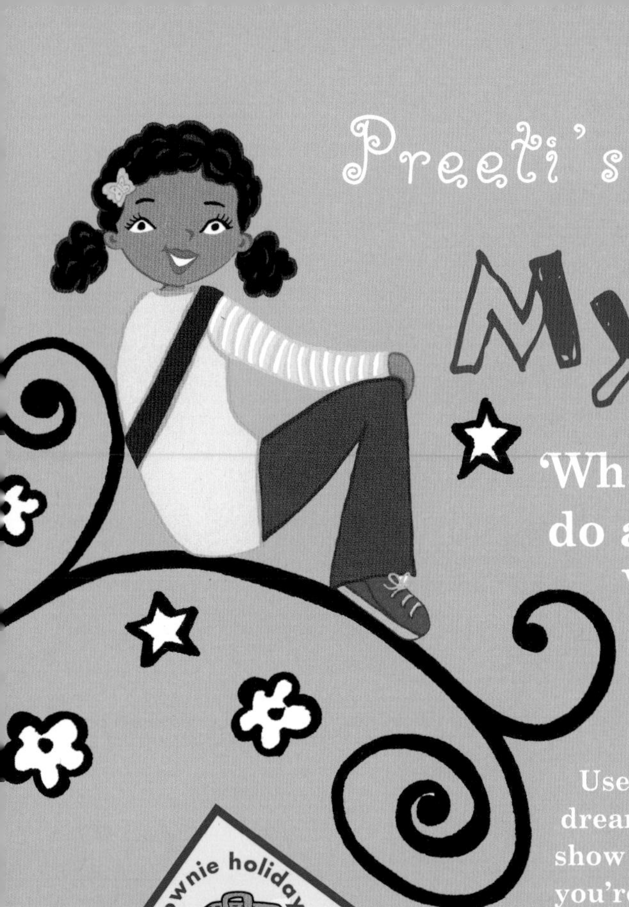

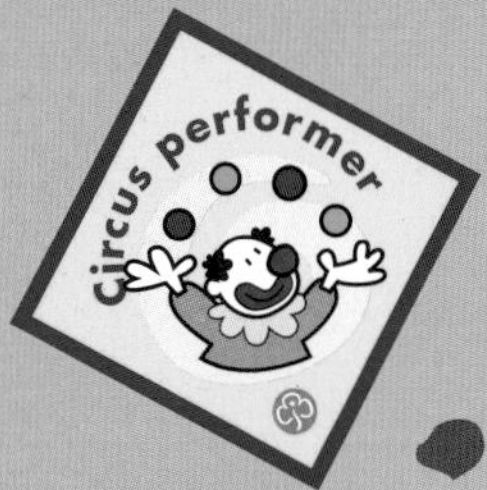
circus performer

My Brownie

'What ten things do you want to do at Brownies before you're ten? Visit another country? Bake a cake? Get the Hobbies badge? Go to Brownie Camp?'

Use these spaces to show your ten must-do Brownie dreams. Draw, write or stick pictures in the spaces to show what you'd like to achieve at Brownies before you're old enough to move to Guides.

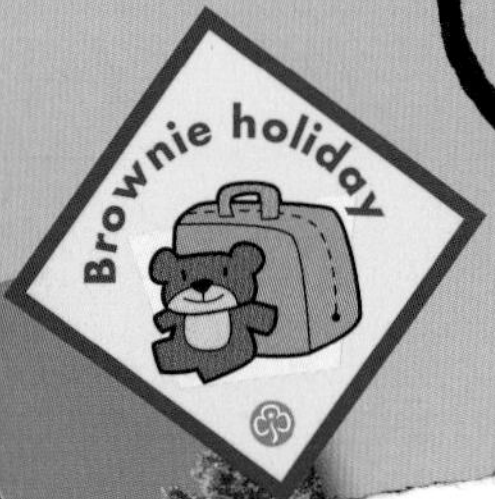
Brownie holiday

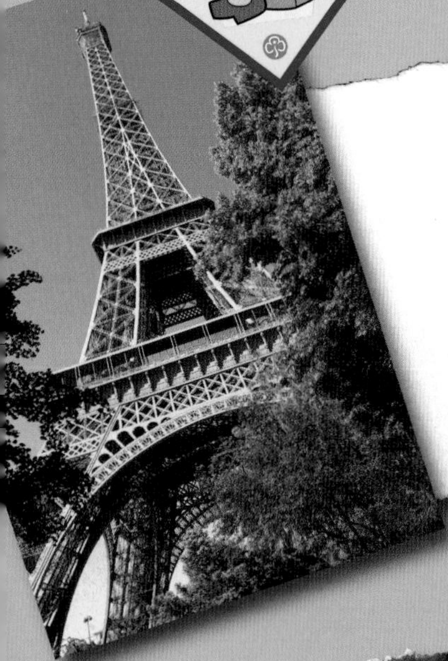

1

2

3

4

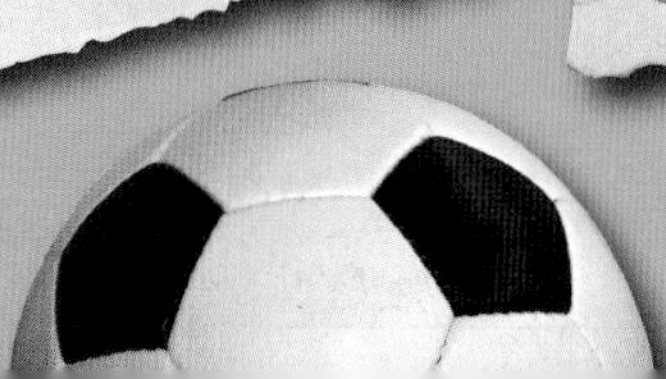

dreams

5

6

8

7

10

9

Out and about

11

Little lost owl

Once, not so very long ago, an owl laid an egg...

It was a cold autumn night when the owl laid her egg. A storm had blown in from the ocean, across the mountains, and shook the branches of the little tree she called home. She nestled down as deep as she could into her cosy nest in an old tree stump and brooded over her new egg.

The seasons changed from autumn to winter. The leaves turned from red to gold, then brown before falling to the ground around the nest. Then the snow came, blanketing the whole island in drifts and ice. All the time the little owl never left her egg, until one day CRACK the egg broke apart and a baby chick came cheeping into the world. The owl was overjoyed to see her baby hatch and spread her wings wide over her, shielding her from the snow and cold.

One day, a little later, the baby owl woke up, all alone in the nest. Her mother was nowhere to be seen.

'Mama?' she cried out, looking around.

She poked her tiny beak from the nest and looked out at the wintry scene. The trees were heavy with snow, red berries glistened on the holly. Still, the little owl couldn't see her mum.

Suddenly there was a rustling in the tree tops. The baby owl craned her tiny head up to see. Something flashed through the branches, followed by a loud crack and a panicked yelp. FLUMP! Something landed in the snow.

Baby owl wobbled from her nest and crunched her way softly across the snow towards the fresh hole formed by the falling red object. She peered into the hole.

'Hello?' she called, then, uncertainly, 'Mama?'

'Ow!' returned a cheery voice from the hole. 'My head!'

A scrabbling noise was followed by the sound of crumbling snow as a smiling red face popped out.

'Allo!' said the creature smiling widely. 'I'm Chuck, the squirrel.'

'Oh!' said the baby owl puzzled. 'I'm... I'm....'

But she realised she didn't know what to say.

'You're an owl,' said Chuck, dusting powdery snow from his nose. 'And your name is?'

'I don't know,' said the baby owl, suddenly feeling very sad. 'I don't think I have a name.'

'Don't be silly,' chuckled Chuck, 'everyone has a name.'

'I don't have one!' said the baby owl. 'And I've lost my mummy!'

With that she burst into tears.

'There, there,' said Chuck, wrapping a friendly paw round her shoulders, 'Let's go to see Angus. He'll know what to do.'

So off they went together, under the snow-covered bushes and over icy roots, until they arrived at a big, round hole underneath the

Illustrated by Ana Bermejo

oldest tree in the wood. Chuck scampered up the tree, sending a shower of pine cones raining down on the ground around the hole.

'Hey, Angus!' shouted Chuck from deep within the branches. 'Wakey, wakey!'

The baby owl tried to hide behind a pile of leaves as she heard a rumbling deep under the ground. Her eyes stretched as a big black and white head appeared from the hole.

'Chuck, is that you? You cheeky rascal!' growled the beast, glowering around him.

'It is!' said Chuck grinning as he dangled upside down from a nearby branch. 'Oops!' he shrieked as he lost his footing and plunged head first into a snowdrift.

'This better be good,' grumbled the monster as he strode menacingly over to Chuck. 'You know I don't like getting up in the winter.'

'It is!' said Chuck, sticking his head out of the snow. 'I've a visitor you really must meet.'

The monster turned grumpily and spied the baby owl looking tiny and afraid behind the pile of leaves. The Angus monster's face softened and he sighed softly.

'Hello, little one,' he murmured, advancing towards the baby owl. 'Don't be afraid, I'm sorry to be a grump but this thoughtless squirrel causes me no end of problems.' He waved a paw despairingly towards Chuck.

The monster reached out a paw, and gently scooped up the baby owl.

'I'm Angus,' said Angus, 'and I'm a badger.'

'I'm an owl,' replied the baby owl, 'and I don't have a name. Or a mummy.'

'Oh, little one, don't be sad,' said Angus, wrapping her warmly in his paw. 'I know all the creatures of the wood. I've lived here such a very long time. I know you have a mummy. I know you have a name. And I know how to make all this right.'

With that, he put the baby owl on his back and took her all the way back through the wood, with Chuck bounding along behind. Eventually, they came to the baby owl's nest and there, frantic with worry, was her mother, hopping round and round in circles.

'Eva!' called her mother joyfully. 'Wherever did you get to? I left you sleeping happily and went to get you breakfast. But when I got back you were gone! I know you're old enough now to leave the nest on your own, how quickly you've grown but how happy I am to see you back!'

And with that Eva jumped from Angus' back and fluttered into her mother's waiting wings.

That night, they cuddled up together in their warm nest as the winds howled and tugged at the trees above. From that day on, Eva always knew who she was.

21

Where would we bee without ☀ honey?

'Honey is a natural sweetener, used for centuries in cooking and medicine. How much do you know about where it comes from?'

HONEYBEE FRIEND

Honeybees are in trouble. As well as climate change and the chemicals used in farming, a bee virus has killed lots of bee colonies. This could have a big impact on us because plants need bees to pollinate them. If there are no bees there would be no plants to feed us. That would mean no wheat to make bread or corn for breakfast cereals. And no fruit or vegetables to keep us healthy.

WHY NOT...

☆ Brush honey on your sausages just before they come out of the oven? Delicious!

☆ Dribble honey over vanilla ice cream?

☆ Stir some honey into hot porridge on a frosty morning?

WHAT'S THE BUZZ?

☆ Bees can fly for up to six miles!

☆ Honey is very soothing for a sore throat.

☆ If a bee collects pollen and nectar from just lavender bushes, its honey tastes of lavender!

SPOT THE DIFFERENCE

Honeybees look very different from the bumblebees you see in parks and gardens. Bumblebees are quite black, big, round and fluffy. Honeybees are a honey colour, not very hairy and quite slim. Don't swat one thinking it's a wasp – honeybees are very important to all of us!

Bumblebee   Honeybee   Wasp

22

Yummy honey cookies

1 Pre-heat the oven to 180°C/350°F/gas mark 4.

2 Cream the butter, sugar and honey until it's pale and fluffy.

3 Sift in the flour along with the ground rice. Mix until you have a dough. Roll out the dough on a floured surface.

4 Use the cutters to make shapes.

5 Place the shapes on greased baking trays. Pop in the oven for 10–15 minutes. Check regularly and cook until golden.

INGREDIENTS (MAKES ABOUT 20)

- ☆ 100g butter plus a little for greasing trays
- ☆ 50g caster sugar
- ☆ 45ml honey
- ☆ 100g plain flour
- ☆ 50g ground rice

YOU WILL NEED

- ☆ mixing bowl
- ☆ wooden spoon
- ☆ rolling pin
- ☆ 2 baking trays
- ☆ biscuit cutters

 **Be safe**

BADGE LINK

Wildlife explorer

Cook

Honey and cinnamon smoothie

INGREDIENTS

- ☆ 1 banana
- ☆ 150ml milk
- ☆ 150g natural yoghurt
- ☆ 45ml honey
- ☆ pinch of cinnamon

YOU WILL NEED

- ☆ knife
- ☆ food processor
- ☆ tall glass

 **Be safe**

Cut your banana into a few pieces. Put all the ingredients into the food processor and whizz until smooth. Pour into a glass and enjoy!

Crazy creature doodle

'Get your dice and pencils ready for a beetle game with a difference. The idea is to create your own special creature!'

YOU WILL NEED

☆ a dice
☆ piece of A4 paper each
☆ pencil each
☆ felt-tip pens, crayons or colouring pencils

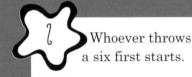
BADGE LINK

Artist

Seasons

Wildlife explorer

Each of the numbers on the dice has a special meaning.

body

head

legs

tail

wings

antennae

1 Whoever throws a six first starts.

2 The first player rolls the dice. To start her creature she must roll a one. If she does, she draws her creature's body on her paper. If she doesn't she hands the dice to the next player.

24

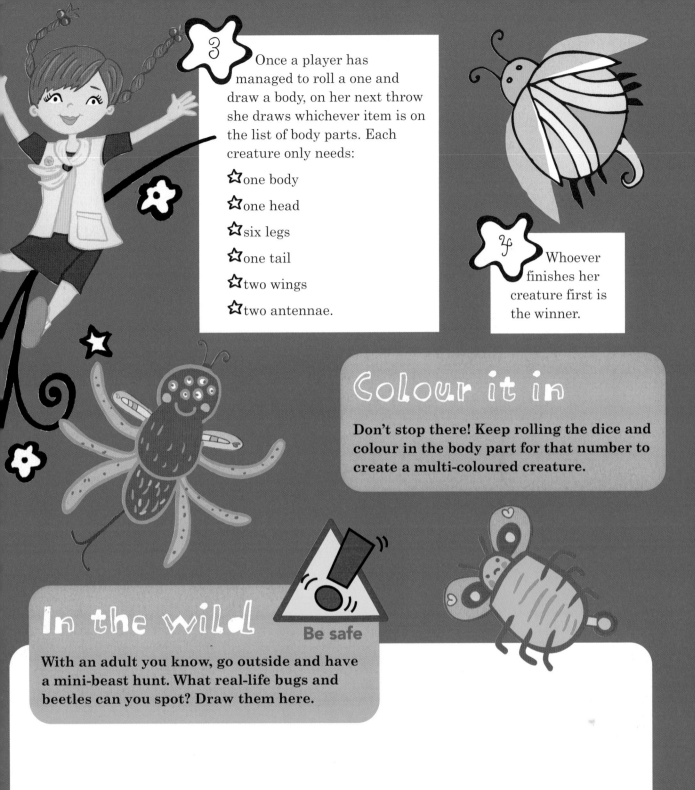

3 Once a player has managed to roll a one and draw a body, on her next throw she draws whichever item is on the list of body parts. Each creature only needs:

- ☆ one body
- ☆ one head
- ☆ six legs
- ☆ one tail
- ☆ two wings
- ☆ two antennae.

4 Whoever finishes her creature first is the winner.

Colour it in

Don't stop there! Keep rolling the dice and colour in the body part for that number to create a multi-coloured creature.

In the wild

Be safe

With an adult you know, go outside and have a mini-beast hunt. What real-life bugs and beetles can you spot? Draw them here.

Ling's crazy craft

Baked beads

'Create your own unique jewellery to wear yourself or give to friends and family.'

Jewel dough

Once you have made this basic recipe, you can design your jewels.

1 Mix the flour and salt. Make a dough by adding the water little by little. The dough must be quite stiff and not sticky.

2 Knead the dough on a lightly floured surface.

BADGE LINK

World cultures

Craft

3 Make beads and other jewel shapes using the ideas opposite.

4 Place the dough shapes on sheets of baking paper.

YOU WILL NEED

☆ 2 cups plain flour, plus extra for kneading

☆ 1 cup salt

☆ 1 cup warm water

☆ bowl

☆ baking paper

⭐ 5 The dough should be baked on the baking paper in a pre-heated oven (120°C/250°F/gas mark ½) for two or more hours. The amount of time depends on the thickness of the dough – larger pieces take longer. Check them regularly to make sure they don't go brown.

Be safe

⭐ 6 Once cool, decorate your items using the ideas below, then use them to create your stunning jewellery.

Decorating

⭐ Glitter mixed into the dough makes super-sparkly jewels.

⭐ Food colouring can be added to the dough before you sculpt it.

⭐ Paint the dough after it's cooked. Let the paint dry then apply a thin coat of PVA glue to seal it.

Beads

Pendants

⭐ 1 Roll out the dough so it's about ½cm thick. Use small biscuit cutters to make pendant shapes. You can also try cutting these by hand.

YOU WILL NEED

⭐ sculpting tools, like a fork, rolling pin, biscuit cutters, toothpicks, rubber stamps, straws, knife

⭐ paper clips

YOU WILL NEED

⭐ skewers

Shape small amounts of dough into balls or ovals. Slide them onto skewers and leave to dry on some baking paper. Remove them from the skewers then place them back on the baking paper to bake.

⭐ 2 Carefully push a paper clip into the back of each shape before baking.

⭐ 27

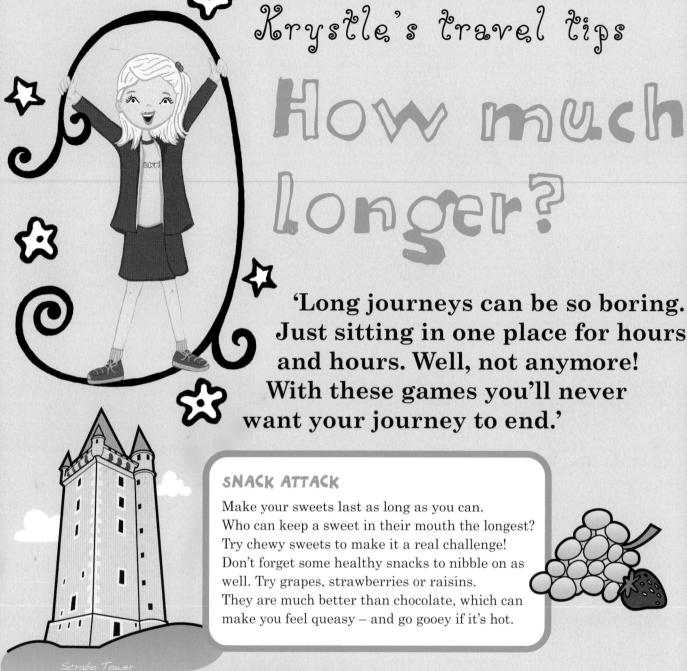

Krystle's travel tips

How much longer?

'Long journeys can be so boring. Just sitting in one place for hours and hours. Well, not anymore! With these games you'll never want your journey to end.'

Scrabo Tower
Northern Ireland

SNACK ATTACK

Make your sweets last as long as you can. Who can keep a sweet in their mouth the longest? Try chewy sweets to make it a real challenge! Don't forget some healthy snacks to nibble on as well. Try grapes, strawberries or raisins. They are much better than chocolate, which can make you feel queasy – and go gooey if it's hot.

QUIET GAME

Who can keep quiet the longest? Laughing counts as noise, so try some sneaky tactics like pulling silly faces at each other – no touching though. Don't utter a sound as you try to catch each other out.

28

NOW YOU SEE IT

One person chooses a distant object that you're travelling towards. The other players close their eyes, and say 'Now!' when they think the car is going past the object. Whose guess was the closest? Try again to see if you can do better.

NAME THAT SOUND

Choose one person to close their eyes for exactly two minutes. Describe to them what you see using noises not words. The person with their eyes closed tries to remember all the things you describe. At the end of the two minutes they tell you everything they can remember.

Agree what noises to use before you play, such as for a caravan, flag, tree or cyclist. There might be too many lorries and cars to point out each one, so look out for motorbikes or pedestrians instead.

Hadrian's Wall
Scotland

BINGO

Before you set off, make bingo sheets for everyone listing things you will see on your journey. The first person to spot them all shouts 'Bingo!' Make a few sheets so you can play again – and on the way home.

NEVER-ENDING STORY

Someone starts the story with a sentence. The next person adds another sentence, and so on until you have created a whole story!

Snowdon Mountain Railway
Wales

ON THE PLATE

Use car registration numbers to make funny sentences.

DE59 HMP Dad Eats Her Majesty's Potatoes

WM10 POL Wallaby Makes 10 Purple Orangutans Laugh

Angel of the North
England

29

Big Brownie sleepover

'These Brownies are on a spooky sleepover at the museum. There are 50 differences between the pictures. Can you spot them all?'

BADGE LINK

Brownie holiday

KEEP SCORE

Use this space to keep a record of how many things you have spotted. Each time you see something, circle it on the picture to the right and keep score here.

Illustrated by Beccy Blake

31

Sally's animal action
Stretch and relax

'Yoga is a great way to relax. Try it on your own, with a friend or as part of your Brownie meeting.'

YOU WILL NEED

Wear loose-fitting clothes and no shoes. A mat is a good idea if the floor is hard – make sure it won't slip.

Web safe

WARM UP

Always warm up before doing yoga. There are some stretches to help with this in the 'Activities' section of **www.girlguiding.org.uk/brownies**.

BrEAThING

Steady breathing is important. Breathe through your nose. Never hold your breath.

BE SAFE

Do not try these activities without asking an adult you know to make sure it's safe.

Be safe

Butterfly

1. Sit on the floor with your back straight. Breathe slowly and deeply.

2. Hold your feet in front of you. Imagine that your legs are wings. Flap them for 20 seconds.

3. Rest with your legs in front of you.

Cat

1 Kneel with your hands on the floor.

2 Breathe out as you slowly arch your back and lower your head.

3 Breathing in, slowly arch your back the other way and lift your head.

4 Repeat three or four times. Sit to rest.

BADGE LINK

Agility   Sports

Lion

1 Kneel on the floor resting on your heels. Place your palms on your thighs. Breathe in.

2 Breathe out. Open your mouth wide. Stick out your tongue! Stretch your eyes and fingers.

3 Breathe in. Pull your tongue back in, close your eyes and relax all over.

4 Repeat three or four times. Take a rest.

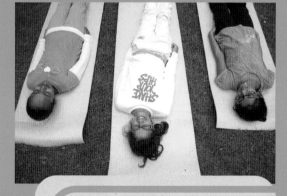

COOL DOWN
Lie quietly for a few minutes to relax. Close your eyes and concentrate on your breathing.

YOGA'S PAST

Thousands of years ago, people in India meditated in the forests. They saw birds and animals stretch to get ready to sleep, and to wake up. These people (yogis) copied the movements and made up their own. Many of the exercises are named after the animals that inspired them.

Web safe

Check out the other great yoga exercises on the Brownies website.

33

Jess's simple science

Light fantastic

'You don't need to be a famous scientist or a fireworks expert to create your own fantastic light show. You just need to make this amazing kaleidoscope!'

YOU WILL NEED

- ☆ A4 sheet of silver mirrorboard (from a craft shop)
- ☆ pencil
- ☆ ruler
- ☆ scissors
- ☆ clear sticky tape
- ☆ cardboard tube about 23cm long
- ☆ black paper
- ☆ cling film
- ☆ a pale-coloured, thin plastic bag
- ☆ sequins, clear beads, coloured confetti
- ☆ 2 rubber bands
- ☆ pens, paints, stickers, glitter and glue to decorate

1 Cut a piece of mirrorboard 23cm long and 10cm wide so it's the same length as the tube.

2 Mark the back of the board in four sections. Score gently along each line with the scissors.

3cm
3cm
3cm
1cm

3 Fold the board to form a triangular prism with the mirrored side on the inside. Secure the 1cm tab with sticky tape.

4 Slide the triangular prism into the tube.

5 On the black paper, draw round the end of the tube. Cut out the circle, pierce a hole in the centre of it then tape it to the tube.

6 Cut out a square of cling film 10cm by 10cm. Secure it over the other end of the tube with a rubber band.

7 Press the centre of the film to make a small pouch. Fill the pouch with beads, sequins or coloured confetti.

8 Cut out two 10cm by 10cm squares from the plastic bag. Secure them over the pouch with a rubber band so none of the beads or sequins can fall out. Decorate your kaleidoscope.

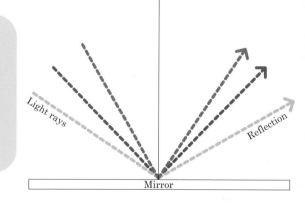

Look through the small hole. Turn it round and round. Watch the colourful patterns form and change.

Sparkly science

How does a kaleidoscope work? Light travels in a straight line. When it bumps into a surface it bounces like a ball bounces off a wall. On most surfaces, light bounces off in all directions. On very shiny surfaces, such as a mirror, it bounces off at the same angle as it hit the surface, showing you a perfect mirror image.

Light rays

Reflection

Mirror

Inside your kaleidoscope the sides of the mirrorboard reflect the beads and sequins. The reflections bounce round all three sides creating lots of identical images. When you turn the kaleidoscope, the sequins and beads move and a different design is reflected.

35

Stars in her eyes

Have you ever wondered what would happen if a character in a story did something differently? Here's your chance to find out.

It's Saturday afternoon and you are in your bedroom getting ready for a very special Brownie event. You've never felt so excited. Your favourite pop star, Diva Diamond, is coming to town and doing a show! You and your Brownie friends are going to see her. And that's not all. Your Brownie Leader, Kay, works at the theatre, so the Brownies have been invited to help her get ready for the show! You really want to get there early so you can pick a fun job…

As you race downstairs, Mum calls, 'Grandad is on the phone. Come and say thank you for the present he sent you.'

You look at the clock. It's time to go. Grandad always chats for hours! **What do you do?**

Talk to your Grandad. ☆ **GO TO STORY A.**

Shout that you are running late and will ring Grandad tomorrow. ☆ **GO TO STORY B.**

STORY A

You just knew it! Grandad talks and talks. By the time you get to the theatre all the other Brownies have beaten you to it. They are busy selling programmes, putting ice creams on trays and getting the drinks ready. Seems like they've got all the fun jobs.

'Hi!' says Kay. 'You've made it. I thought you weren't coming. Everyone else has chosen their jobs already. Let's see, what's left… You can be my odd-job person and help me with all the little last-minute things. OK?'

You are so disappointed. You really wanted to show people to their seats. But Kay soon finds a job for you. You have to wait by the door and take any wheelchair users to the place where they can watch the show.

Soon a group of girls arrive and one of them is in a wheelchair. You offer to show her where to go. On the way, you get chatting.

'Wow, what a great spot,' says the girl. 'I'm right at the front! This is so cool! Thanks. What's your name? I'm Evie.'

Evie's friends go off to get ice cream, so you stay and chat with her. You have a laugh and time flies. At last you say, 'I should get back. Kay might need me.'

'No. Stay and watch the show with us,' says Evie. 'You'll get such a great view from here!'

It's tempting to stay. **What do you do?**

Stay with Evie and her friends. ☆ **GO TO STORY C.**

Go back to Kay. ☆ **GO TO STORY B.**

Illustrated by Cathi Mingus

36

STORY D

Your next job is on the merchandise stall helping to sell T-shirts. You really love the pink ones with 'Diva' on the front in glittery writing. They sell fast and before long there's only one left in your size. It slips down behind a pile of boxes, out of sight.

A girl comes up and asks for that size. If you keep quiet, you might be able to 'find' the last T-shirt later and buy it for yourself. **What do you do?**

Don't say anything.

⭐ **GO TO STORY E.**

Hand over the T-shirt.

⭐ **GO TO STORY G.**

STORY B

You're the first to arrive at the theatre. Kay is waiting with a list of jobs in her hand.

'Hi!' she says. 'As you're the first one here you can pick a job. What would you like to do?'

You decide that showing people to their seats sounds like fun – and it is! You see loads of people you know, and chat to some friends from school. Still, all the time you have a guilty feeling inside – will Grandad be upset because you didn't talk to him? ⭐ **GO TO STORY J.**

STORY C

You decide to hang out with Evie. Together you have lots of fun. Just before the show starts, Kay comes looking for you. ⭐ **GO TO STORY F.**

STORY E

The stallholder says, 'I'm sure we had another one...'

She looks behind the boxes, finds the T-shirt and sells it.

'We need to move all these boxes. They're in the way. Can you help take them outside?' the stallholder asks.

When you get back, Kay is waiting. ⭐ **GO TO STORY F.**

STORY F

'There you are!' says Kay. 'I've been looking for you. I needed someone to take flowers up to Diva's dressing room. Never mind, I did it myself. You'll never guess – I actually talked to her! Anyway, let's find our seats, it's nearly showtime.'

You're so disappointed! ☆ **GO TO STORY J.**

STORY G

You sigh and hand over the T-shirt. A few minutes later Kay comes to get you for your next job.

'Thank you! You've been so helpful,' says the stallholder. 'Here's a little thank you present.'

She pulls a pink T-shirt down from the display and pops it over your head. It's so big it looks like a dress, but you love it!

Kay is holding a huge bunch of flowers and looking very excited.

'These have just arrived for Diva,' she says. 'Can you take them to her dressing room before she goes on stage?'

You can't believe it – if you're quick you might see Diva herself! You grab the flowers and race off. As you tear up the back stairs, you hear a crash and a shriek. Someone has dropped a tray of drinks. Orange juice and ice cubes are spreading all over the floor. It's really dangerous and needs clearing up quickly. But if you stay and help, you might not get to see Diva. **What do you do?**

Stay and help. ☆ **GO TO STORY H.**

Run past with your flowers – you'll help on your way back. ☆ **GO TO STORY I.**

38

STORY H

You carefully put Diva's flowers down and help mop up the spilled drinks. Just then, Diva's band run down the stairs! You can't believe your eyes, but you manage to speak up and warn them about the wet floor.

'Thanks, we could have slipped,' says the drummer. 'Great dress! Do you want it signed?'

All the band quickly sign your T-shirt! You are so thrilled! Now to see Diva herself…

You run to her room with the flowers, but you're too late – she's gone backstage. One of her helpers sees the disappointment in your face. She tells you to take the flowers to your seat and watch the show. You're puzzled, but you do as she says.

The show is amazing! At the end, the helper comes and taps you on the shoulder.

'Take the flowers up on stage for Diva,' she whispers. Next minute, a spotlight is shining on you. You somehow get yourself up on to the stage. It's really hot and the lights are dazzling. Diva smiles at you. You hand her the flowers and hear the crowd roar. Diva gives you a hug and also signs your T-shirt, while your Brownie friends scream and cheer. It's the best moment of your life!

STORY I

You decide you really want to give Diva the flowers. When you reach her dressing room, one of her helpers comes to the door and takes them. You get a glimpse of Diva inside, putting on her make-up. Wow!

You take your seat just as the curtain rises. Diva and her band appear. You notice that the drummer has a bandage round her arm and when she starts playing, you can see she's in pain. Kay whispers that the drummer slipped on some spilled drinks and hurt her wrist. Now you feel really guilty.
☆ GO TO STORY J.

STORY J

At last the show starts, and it's amazing! Diva is fantastic, and she sings all your favourite songs. But you still can't quite shake off the bad feeling inside, and it spoils your fun. You wish you could go back and do things differently…

BADGE LINK

Writer

39

Ling's wildlife watch

Nature detective

'Wherever you live one thing's for certain – there's wildlife all about you! All you need to do is look closely for the evidence.'

BADGE LINK

Wildlife explorer

Seasons

CLUES TO LOOK FOR

Can you spot the signs that wildlife has been about? Keep your eyes and ears open. Are those paw tracks? Are there nests in the hedge? Is that a fox on the pavement? Would you know an ants' nest if you saw one?

HABITS AND HABITATS

Can you work out whether animals, insects or birds have certain habits? For example, which bird is always first at the feeder? Do you notice when the hedgehogs go into hibernation? When did the swallows return for the summer?

LOOK OUT!

Use these signs to keep a record of some of the creatures you see. Add two of your own special animal sightings at the end.

Creature	Evidence	Name and details	Where you saw it	Time and date spotted
		Duck		
		Squirrel		
		Fox		
		Pet dog		
		Snail		
		Spider		

NATURE DIARY

Keep a diary with notes of when you see creatures or evidence of wildlife. If you see something that you don't recognise, make a sketch of it or take a quick photo if you can. Look it up later in a reference book or online.

NATURE RAMBLE

Be safe

Why not ask your Leader if you and your Brownie friends can go for a walk? It is surprising how different the wildlife is in different areas. Look out for animal tracks that you might not find in your garden or local park.

39

Krystle's friend facts
What's in a name?

'Did you know that behind many names is a special meaning? We got a group of Brownie friends together to find out what their names mean.'

CHLOE

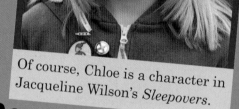

Chloe comes from the Greek word for young green shoot or plant.

Of course, Chloe is a character in Jacqueline Wilson's *Sleepovers*.

EMILY

Hi! My name comes from the Latin word for rival.

Famous Emilys include Emily Brontë, the author of *Wuthering Heights*, and actor Emily Blunt.

BADGE LINK

Computer   World cultures

JASMINE

Jasmine is a Persian name taken from the flower with the same name.

Jasmine is the name of one of the main characters in the Disney film *Aladdin*.

GRACE

My name means 'effortless beauty' in Latin.

The heroine Grace Darling and the actor Grace Kelly, who became Princess Grace of Monaco, are famous Graces.

42

MY NAME

Want to know what your name means? Use this space to find out about your name and the names of some of your Brownie friends. Do you know anyone famous with the same name?

NAME	MEANING	FAMOUS PEOPLE

ISABELLA

The name Isabella is a popular royal name. In 2007, the Crown Prince and Crown Princess of Denmark named their daughter Isabella.

Hello. My name comes from the name Elizabeth. It means 'My God is a vow' or 'My God is an oath'.

Go online and put your name into **www.wikipedia.org** or try baby-naming websites such as **www.babynames.co.uk** or **www.bounty.com/baby-names** to find out more.

Web safe

OTHER NAMES

It isn't just girls' names that have meanings. Boys' names do, too! Last names can mean something as well. And place names often have a link to old local words or customs.

43

Making signs

'Do you take chatting with your friends for granted? Do you pick up the phone for a natter without thinking about it? What if you couldn't hear very well? How would you communicate then?'

BADGE LINK
Communicator
Disability awareness

IF YOU'VE GOT SOMETHING TO SAY, SIGN IT!
Use sign language with your friends!

GOOD MORNING!

Goodbye

GOOD

HELLO

PLEASE

Thank you

WELL DONE

Good luck

HOME

WALK

Bicycle

WHO?

WHAT?

PLAY

Where?

DID YOU KNOW...

☆ There are over 45,000 deaf children in the UK?

☆ Thousands of deaf children use sign language?

☆ 16,316 Girlguiding UK members learned how to sign the Promise in 2009?

☆ Lots of deaf children have a special sign language name? This is sometimes their favourite colour, hobby or food.

ndcs
every deaf child

The National Deaf Children's Society (NDCS) is a charity that helps deaf children and their families. It does this in many ways including having a Listening Bus. The bus travels round the UK visiting schools and youth clubs so that young people can learn more about deafness and also see some of the technology which deaf children use. Vibrating alarm clocks and video telephones are just some of the things deaf children can use.

NDCS wants to help deaf children enjoy all the same fun activities that hearing children do, like playing sports and going to Brownies. If you'd like to help deaf children why not sign up for Sign It! – a sponsored sign language event. It's a fab way to learn some sign language and help raise money for NDCS. To find out more, visit **www.ndcs.org.uk/guides**.

Web safe

Sally's sewing skills...

Sock it!

'Are you the proud owner of an MP3 player, iPod or mobile phone? Want to keep it nice and shiny? Have a go at making these great bags – for yourself or as a present.'

Sock shock

YOU WILL NEED
- ☆ an old, clean sock
- ☆ scissors
- ☆ needle and thread
- ☆ piece of wool
- ☆ small safety pin
- ☆ toggle and beads

1. Cut straight across at the heel of the sock. Turn it inside out and sew across.

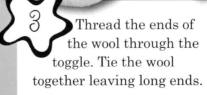

2. Make a small snip in the cuff of the sock. Thread the wool through the cuff.

3. Thread the ends of the wool through the toggle. Tie the wool together leaving long ends.

4. Thread two or three beads on to each strand. Knot the wool.

- ☆ If there isn't a cuff on your sock, make one by turning the top inside and sewing neatly.
- ☆ Use a trainer sock if you have one. You won't have to cut the toe off!

46

Felt envelope

YOU WILL NEED
- ☆ felt
- ☆ ruler and pencil
- ☆ scissors
- ☆ thick thread or wool
- ☆ needle and pins
- ☆ sequins, beads and ribbon
- ☆ press-popper or button
- ☆ fabric glue (optional)

1 Measure the phone or player. Mark out a piece of felt twice the length and at least a centimetre wider on either side. Add more for a fold-over flap if you want. Cut it out.

2 Loosely pin the felt in place. Decide how you'll decorate it. Draw your design on the felt.

3 Unpin the felt and sew on any ribbon, sequins and beads you want.

4 Loosely pin the felt back in shape. Securely sew the sides.

5 Sew a loop and button or press-popper in place.

TOP TIP
Use fabric glue to stick sequins and felt in place before sewing them.

Woolly warmer

YOU WILL NEED
- ☆ knitting needles and ball of wool
- ☆ darning needle
- ☆ scissors
- ☆ ribbon

1 Cast on enough stitches to allow for the width of the phone or player with at least a centimetre either side.

2 Keep knitting until it is over twice the length of the player or phone. Cast off.

3 Sew up the sides. Sew a piece of ribbon to the top that will loop all the way round.

BADGE LINK
Craft
Designer
Brownie skills

47

Isobel's big move

Isobel and her family are moving house – all the way to Egypt!

AT HOME WITH MUM AND BROTHER

But where will our new home be, Mum?

In Cairo – that's the capital of Egypt.

Wow! That's exciting.

But where will we go to school?

Don't worry Isobel, there's a school very close to our new home. You'll soon make lots of new friends.

It'll be sunny and hot in Egypt.

I know. It's not going to be like home.

We might even have our own camel!

I don't want to move.

LATER AT BROWNIES

So, does anybody have any news to share?

Er, I do.

48

Jess's brain bender!

Brainteasing bugs

'How much do you know about butterflies, bugs and other mini-beasts? Test your knowledge here!'

CREEPY-CRAWLY CROSSWORD

Double fun with this crossword. Look at the ladybirds in the grid and see if you can spot the odd one out.

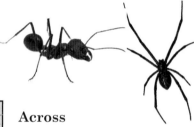

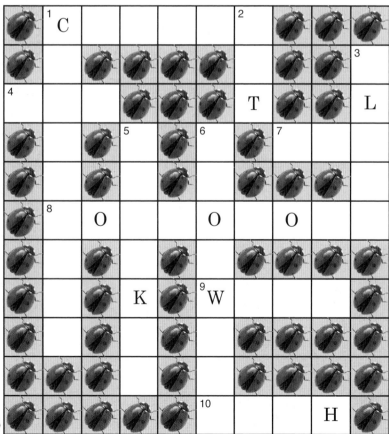

Across
1. A caterpillar's home when it's turning into a butterfly.
4. Lives in a colony under a hill.
7. Makes honey?
8. The black widow is this type of spider.
9. Stripy like a bee but it can sting more than once.
10. Like a butterfly but not quite as pretty.

Down
1. A hundred legs to help it walk.
2. A tiny egg – the larva of a louse. They can live in your hair. Yuk!
3. Will make your cat or dog scratch like mad!
5. A jumping insect with the same name as a sport.
6. A bright bug in the dark.

MIXED UP MINI-BEASTS

Unscramble the letters to work out the names of these mini-beasts.

1. YFL
2. MORW
3. IPERDS
4. TEELEB
5. BAYIDRDL

BUTTERFLY HUNT

Hunt up, down and diagonally in the grid for the butterflies named below.

Blue
Brown
Comma
Snout
White
Admiral
Copper
Buckeye
Monarch
Peacock
Ringlet
Sulphur
Hackberry
Orange tip
Hairstreak

A	B	B	S	B	L	U	E	O	H	H
R	R	C	N	C	A	I	S	R	A	A
I	O	E	O	O	O	A	U	A	C	I
N	W	R	U	M	D	P	L	N	K	R
G	N	H	T	M	O	E	P	G	B	S
L	B	R	I	A	P	A	H	E	E	T
E	N	R	E	T	A	C	U	T	R	R
T	A	U	N	S	E	O	R	I	R	E
L	M	O	N	A	R	C	H	P	Y	A
K	H	P	B	U	C	K	E	Y	E	K

WORM'S EYE VIEW

Help Wendy Worm find her way from her underground home to the juicy apples on the ground.

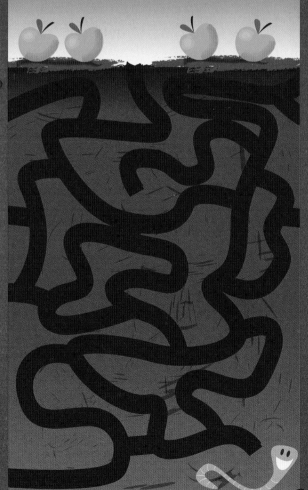

BADGE LINK

seasons

Wildlife explorer

53

Competition

Love a good read? If yes, tell us about Brownies and win a set of fabulous Brownie books!

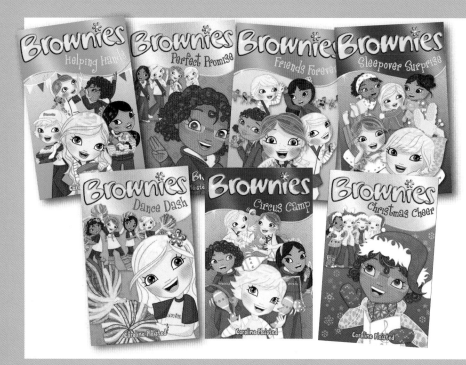

We have three sets of the terrific Brownies series by Caroline Plaisted to give away to three bookworms. What's more, Caroline will be signing each and every one of her books for our lucky winners. For a chance to be one of them just write in to us with your list of '10 top things at Brownies'.

You can buy your own copies of these fabulous books from Girlguiding UK Trading Sevice for only £3.50 each.

So, be one of our winners and meet best friends Katie, Ellie, Charlie, Jamila and Grace – and find out all about their Brownie adventures in all seven books!

COMPETITION RULES

Write your list of '10 top things at Brownies'.

On the back of your list write:

☆ your name

☆ your age

☆ your address

☆ your Brownie unit

☆ the three best things in your *Brownie Annual 2011*.

Send your entry to:
Brownie Annual 2011 Competition
Girlguiding UK
17–19 Buckingham Palace Road
London SW1W 0PT

The closing date for the competition is 28 February 2011 – so get writing!

If you would like to know more about Caroline Plaisted and her Brownies series visit **www.stripespublishing.co.uk**.

Brownie shopping

There are lots of brilliant Brownie gifts available – these are just a few of them!

MUG
2388 £2.50
£2.55

EARRINGS*
7411 £4   £4.09

BROWNIE CLIPS
2602 Teddy
7116 Monkey
Height 8cm
£3 EACH
£3.06

BROWNIE PHOTO FRAME
7388 £4
£4.09

Photo size 6" x 4"

FLOWER TOP PEN
7130 £2.75
£2.81

DAYSACK
8700 £8
£8.17

Image shown is larger than actual size.

PYJAMAS
100% Cotton
£15

SHORTIE PYJAMAS AND FLUFFY DRESSING GOWN ALSO AVAILABLE

ORDER CODES				
CHILD AGE	6-7	8-9	10-11	12-13
PYJAMAS	8114	8115	8116	8117

Prices in black are valid from 1 September 2010. The red prices reflect the higher rate of VAT applied to relevant products from 4 January 2011 onwards.

Three easy ways to shop

for all your guiding wear, books and gifts

Girlguiding UK
Trading Service

OPEN

At our volunteer shops (Depots)
Ring 0161 941 2237
to find your nearest one

@
www.girlguidingukshop.co.uk
Shop online day or night

Guiding Essentials catalogue
Phone 0161 941 2237
Fax 0161 941 6326

The mouse of

A tale of tongue twisters and ogres!

There once lived a mouse next to a deep, dark forest
called Alphabet Wood.
Beyond this forest lay the Mountain of Cheese
that smelled ever so good.
But in Alphabet Wood lived three ogres
so terrifyingly monstrous,
That to come across even one of them
would be truly disastrous.

Every day Mouse would look longingly
at the Mountain of Cheese,
With nothing more than dried biscuit
to help his hunger pangs ease.
Then one day a strong gust of wind
brought a particularly strong scent,
Of Cheddar, Gouda, Emmental, Brie and all things
Mouse thought of as heavenly sent.

'That's it!' exclaimed Mouse, 'I can resist it no more
– to that mountain I must go!'
And packing his biscuits he went into Alphabet Wood
without further ado.
For hours Mouse travelled the woods,
untroubled by creature or ogre.
Suddenly a voice spoke, and poor Mouse squealed with fright,
'Oh, no, it's all over!'

'Too-whit-awhoo,' said the voice, 'who goes there
and what do you have with you?'
'Oh, it's you, Owl!' said Mouse relieved.
'It's only I, Mouse, passing through.'
'Mouse, you know better than to wander
these dangerous woods,' scolded Owl.
'Three hungry ogres are about, their appetites great,
and tempers foul.

'But I will help you – I will tell you a secret,
in exchange for some biscuit.'
'That's fair,' replied Mouse, and gave up a biscuit
in exchange for a secret.
'If you encounter an ogre,' whispered Owl,
'It will ask you for a tongue twister.
'For these ogres are quite peculiar,
and love all things rhyme, lyrical and clever.'

Illustrated by Ana Bermejo

56

alphabet wood

'So choose your answer well,
for if your words fail to satisfy the ogre,
'Then, I'm afraid to say, that of you there will be...
nothing but a little leftover.'
Heeding Owl's words Mouse journeyed
deeper into Alphabet Wood,
And, lo and behold, it was not long
before a terrible ogre in his path stood.

she sells sea shells

'Who goes there?' screamed the ogre. 'Feed me a tongue twister,
or I'll eat you instead!'
'Sh-sh-she sells sea shells by the seashore.
Th-th-these shells she sells are sea shells, I'm sure,' Mouse said.
'Oh, that was clever,' said the ogre, 'but you will have to do better
if you meet my sister.'
And with that Mouse passed safely through, his heartbeat quicker,
and his footsteps faster.

And it was not long before he encountered a second ogre
– bigger, louder and far, far uglier.
'Who goes there?' bellowed the ogre. 'Feed me a tongue twister,
or you'll be my supper!'
'Peter Piper picked a peck of pickled peppers. Did Peter Piper
pick a peck of pickled peppers?' Mouse squealed.
'If Peter Piper picked a peck of pickled peppers, where's the peck
of pickled peppers Peter Piper picked?'

by the seashore

'Oh, that was delightful,' said the ogre, 'but you must do better
if you meet our mother.'
And so Mouse passed safely through, each step drawing him closer,
and the smell of cheese getting stronger.
Finally, Mouse came across the last ogre
– biggest, loudest and ugliest of the three.
'Who goes there?' roared the ogre. 'Feed me a tongue twister,
or my meal you will be!'

'Betty Botter bought some butter.
"But," she said, "this butter's bitter. If I bake this bitter butter, it
will make my batter bitter.
"But a bit of better butter would make my batter better."
So she bought a bit of butter, better than her bitter butter,
and she baked it in her batter, and the batter was not bitter.'
'Oh, that was exquisite,' said the ogre, 'through the Wood you're free,
to come and go as you feel.'
With a hop, skip and spring in his step, Mouse left the woods behind,
his dreams of the Mountain of Cheese now finally real.

Love hearts

'Weave heart-shaped baskets to give to someone special – maybe on a special occasion!'

YOU WILL NEED

- ☆ sheets of A4 paper (different colours)
- ☆ ruler
- ☆ pencil
- ☆ compass or protractor
- ☆ scissors
- ☆ ribbon or string

BADGE LINK
Craft GLUE

1 Take one sheet of paper and fold it in half.

3 Draw two lines across the box, top to bottom, to make three 3cm strips.

2 In one corner against the folded edge, draw a 9cm square.

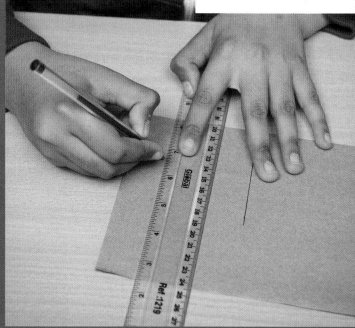

4 Draw a semicircle on the top of the box.

5 Cut out the shape.

Be safe

6 Cut along the two lines going through the box, and about 3–4mm past the ends.

7 With a different coloured piece of paper, repeat steps 1 to 6.

8 Weave the two shapes together. Take the top strip of one shape and weave it through the strips of the other shape. Do the same with the middle strip and finally the bottom strip.

9 If you've done it successfully you should have a little heart basket.

10 Create a hole at the top of the heart. Thread the string or ribbon through and make a hanging loop.

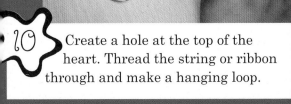

Make more heart baskets in different colours. Add some decoration – use your imagination! Think paint, sequins, tinsel, glitter, googly eyes and feathers. What about something special to put inside them? Turn the page for some yummy ideas!

Krystle's tasty treats

Sweets in a jiffy

'Two very easy-to-make treats. Great for a present, or to enjoy with friends. Yum!'

Fudge

INGREDIENTS
- ☆ 100g butter
- ☆ 400g can of condensed milk
- ☆ 1 teaspoon of vanilla extract
- ☆ 800g icing sugar

1 Whisk the butter, condensed milk and vanilla extract together.

YOU WILL NEED
- ☆ mixing bowl
- ☆ electric whisk
- ☆ baking tin
- ☆ baking paper
- ☆ knife
- ☆ chopping board
- ☆ cling film

2 Add the icing sugar little by little. Whisk to form a dough-like mixture.

3 Line the tin with baking paper. Press the mixture into the tin, making a nice even surface.

BADGE LINK
Cook

4 Mark the fudge into pieces. Leave it to set in the fridge for four hours.

5 Once set, cut the fudge in to pieces. Wrap them in cling film ready to give away.

Be safe

Turkish delight

YOU WILL NEED

- ☆ saucepan, ideally with a heavy base
- ☆ ladle
- ☆ baking tin
- ☆ baking paper
- ☆ chopping board
- ☆ airtight container

INGREDIENTS

- ☆ 250ml water
- ☆ 25g gelatine* powder
- ☆ 4 teaspoons of rose water
- ☆ 450g caster sugar
- ☆ icing sugar

* vegetarian gelatine is available in larger supermarkets and health food shops

1 Mix the water, gelatine powder, rose water and caster sugar in the pan.

2 Over a low heat, stir until all the sugar and gelatine has dissolved.

3 Bring to the boil without stirring. Reduce the heat and simmer for 20–25 minutes.

6 Pour the mixture into the tin. Leave to cool then put in fridge overnight to set.

4 Remove from the heat and leave to cool for a few minutes.

5 Line the tin with lightly greased baking paper.

7 Once set, cut it into square pieces.

Ask an adult to show you how to use the whisk safely and to help you heat the Turkish delight.

Be safe

8 Coat the pieces in icing sugar. Store in an airtight container.

True tales

These are the amazing winners of the 2010 *Brownie Annual* competition. The guiding stories they have gathered are all real!

STAR INTERVIEWERS

We received so many excellent entries that we selected four winners!

☆ Emily (aged 9) of 14th City of Coventry South Brownies interviewed her Mum, who was a Brownie in the 1970s.

☆ Rebecca (aged 9) of 1st Horseheath Brownies interviewed her Godmother, Auntie Grace, who was a Guide in the 1950s and 1960s.

☆ Alice (aged 7 and 5 months) of 1st Woodborough Brownies interviewed her Great Auntie Barbara, who was a Brownie during the Second World War!

☆ Grace (aged 10) of 1st Hornchurch Brownies did two interviews. She found out about her aunt being a Brownie in the 1950s, and her Mum being a Brownie in the 1970s.

Read on to see what Emily, Rebecca, Alice and Grace found out for us about guiding back then.

ITCHY CLOTHING!

Emily   'She had to wear a brown dress, a yellow tie, a belt and a woolly bobble hat. My Mum never liked the bobble hat, she wanted a beret!'

Rebecca   'Back in 1959 the Guide uniform was very strict and included a very itchy navy beret and skirt.'

Grace   'They wore a brown dress that went down to the knees, which was secured by a brown leather belt.'

STRICT RULES!

Emily   'My Mum had to keep 2p in her pocket (in case she ever needed to make an emergency phone call from a phone box), a pencil, a safety pin and a piece of string.'

Rebecca   'Every week they would have an inspection to check the contents of their pockets and the reef knot at the back of their ties.'

Grace   'Their Brownie badge had a picture of a Brownie on it, and it was made of metal which had to be polished. Brown Owl inspected this every week.'

62

FAVOURITE ACTIVITY...

Emily   'My Mum's favourite activity was camping.'

Rebecca   'Her favourite activity was camping.'

Alice   'She told me so many stories about camping. She has been on 175 camping trips over 45 years in guiding!'

Grace   'They had to make a bed rack out of wood, and hang the meat in a meatsafe up in the trees. They cooked over a campfire and heated water in a dustbin to wash. The toilets at camp were emptied into a pit. At one camp, a girl fell in!'

CAMPING CAPERS!

Emily   'She remembers making gadgets. She made a sink unit out of wood by lashing sticks together. She also made a tiny raft with a candle that floated on the river. They all looked lovely as they were lit and floated off into the distance.'

Rebecca   'One group came over in a dreadful state and said they could hear heavy breathing outside their tent. Auntie Grace went to sort it out and her foot made contact with a hedgehog, which rolled itself up in a ball so that she [accidentally] kicked it inside the tent. The hedgehog was the cause of the heavy breathing. She caught it and let it go on the Scout site next door!'

Alice   'They walked along the beach and suddenly they were stuck in heavy rain with nowhere to go. They ran to a café but it was only 8.15am and it didn't open until 10am. However, the lady inside let them in because they were absolutely drenched! She gave them all leftover cakes and buns, which must have been very exciting!'

FACT BOX

A gadget was a useful item made out of sticks and string. At camp, Guides made gadgets such as wellie racks.

Did you enjoy reading what our star interviewers had to reveal? Then visit **www.girlguiding.org.uk/centenary/storybank** for more guiding stories. You can read the full stories from Emily, Rebecca, Alice and Grace there, too!

Web safe

Preeti's creative challenge

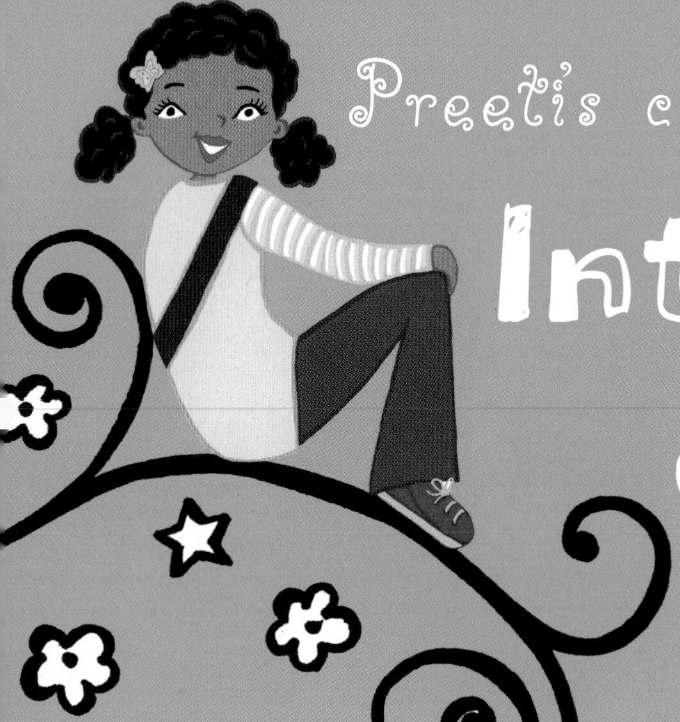

Interior designer

'Are you the next Cath Kidston or Laura Ashley? Let your design skills flow and create your dream bedroom.'

YOU WILL NEED

- ✩ tape measure
- ✩ pencils, pens and paper
- ✩ calculator
- ✩ catalogues and brochures
- ✩ scissors

1 Measure your room. How long is it? How wide is it? Use the grid to show how big it is – each square could be 25cm. Mark where the windows and doors are.

2 **What will you need in your bedroom? A wardrobe? Drawers? Desk for doing homework? Don't forget the bed!**

3 Look for curtains, lights and duvet covers, too. Don't forget to pick colours for the walls. What about a mural?

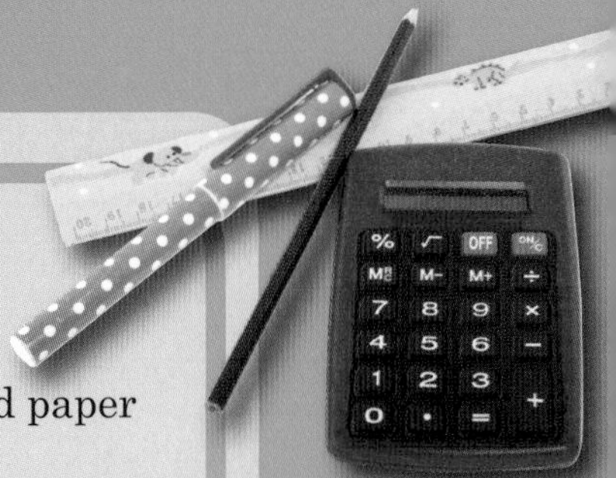

What's your style?

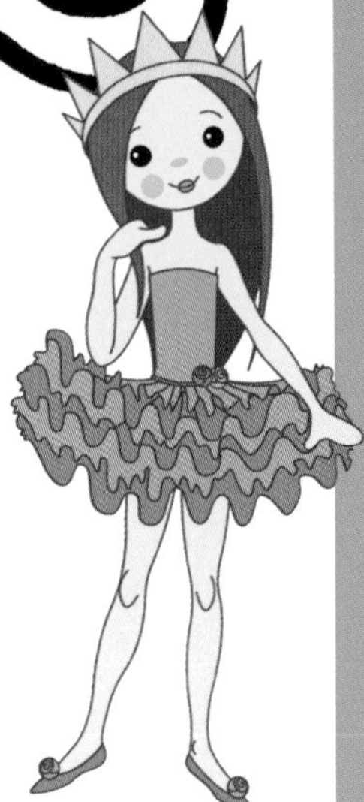

- ✩ Are you pink and glittery with a passion for being a princess?
- ✩ Are you a techno girl into computer games?
- ✩ How about a sporty theme?
- ✩ Will you have a Brownie bedroom?
- ✩ Are you bold and bright and just love lots of colour?
- ✩ Are flowers and butterflies your style?

Do you share your room? What areas can you decorate? Look at catalogues and online for ideas. Cut out pictures of the things you like. Check how big they are. Use the pictures – or draw your own – to create your bedroom design below. **Go on – get designing.**

Web safe

BADGE LINK

Designer

Number fun

Craft

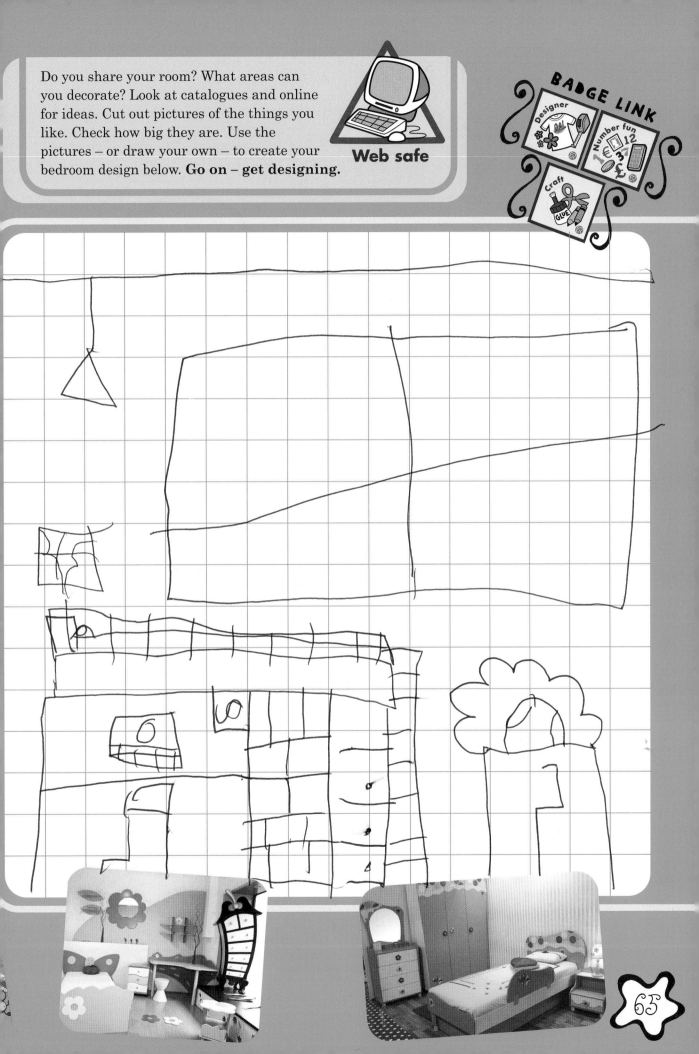

Sally's guide to Guides

The Adventure is ON!

'I'm almost ten. And I'm about to have a real adventure finding out about Guides.'

CRACK THE CODE

A mysterious email has landed in Sally's inbox... The message is scrambled. She needs your help to crack the code so she can read the message.

ZDeyar XSawllvy,

Yuout're sinrviqtepd too vnismit L15lth zPoiweqll

HGugidfes enedxt CWebdnaeszdayy

fxrowm 1g9.3f0 tto 2y1.0u0 hdouwrs.

PSo ofanr tmhils tjerkm, wie'vhe bgeefn

geetdticng balal czrevatxivwe dvoiung tousr

Arrtqispts obandgme, alnd klejarinihng

gabfouet tdhe cenbviaroznmyenxt wwitvh

Guo Ftor SIt! RGRQRRPeeon.

Wne'rme llookkijng ifohrwgarfd teo odur

canbnuaal ZPaytrxol wcovokuintg

csomrpeqtiptioon nat mthle eknd jof itehrm,

ganfd aere dbucsy bplaanzniyng

xwhwat vwe'ure tgosinrg tqo

gpet oup nto mon loukr sjumimehr cgamfp.

Wee cdanc't wbaiat tzo myeext ywouv!

Fruom,

TPusffrin QPaptrool

Illustrated by Bill Ledger

MEET THE PUFFINS

On Sally's visit she meets the Puffin Patrol. Unfortunately, she's muddled up their names. Can you help her remember who's who?

Jo   Hannah   Becky   Emily   Aicha

GUIDE CAMP

Sally's invited to visit the Puffin Patrol at the summer camp. At midnight, everyone renews their Promise. Sally says her Brownie Promise along with them. It's the best bit so far! When she shows her Six the photos afterwards, they see there were lots of others having fun at Guide camp! How many creatures can you spot in the photo?

FIND OUT MORE

☆ Try 'Brownies Go For It!' in *Brownies Adventure On*.

☆ Visit **www.girlguiding.org.uk/guides**.

☆ Play the 'Detective Brownie' game on the Brownie website – go to **www.girlguiding.org.uk/brownies**.

☆ Ask your Leader if you can visit Guides.

☆ Is there a Pack Leader helping at Brownies? Ask her what Guides is like!

Web safe

67

Jess's great grub
Picnic hamper

'Having a picnic outside is a tradition going back hundreds of years. Why not organise one with your friends?'

BLT wrap

Eight yummy mini-wraps of the classic bacon, lettuce and tomato (BLT) sandwich.

INGREDIENTS
☆ 2 slices of bacon
☆ half a lettuce
☆ 1 tomato
☆ 4 flour tortillas
☆ mayonnaise

YOU WILL NEED
☆ knife and chopping board
☆ cocktail sticks

1 Chop the bacon into strips. Place them carefully under a hot grill. Cook until they are brown and a bit crispy.

Be safe

2 Tear up the lettuce. Carefully slice the tomato.

3 Spread each tortilla with a little mayonnaise, then top each one with bacon, lettuce and tomato.

4 Fold the sides of the tortilla over, then roll it up. Do all four tortillas.

5 Cut the wraps in half. Stick a cocktail stick in each wrap to stop it unfolding in your picnic basket.

Pink fizz

A cool fizzy drink perfect for a hot summer day.

INGREDIENTS (MAKES ONE LITRE)
☆ 5 unwaxed lemons
☆ 200g raspberries
☆ 200g caster sugar
☆ 750ml sparkling water

YOU WILL NEED
☆ knife
☆ food processor
☆ sieve
☆ large jug
☆ spoon

Be safe

1 Cut the lemons in half and remove any pips you can see.

2 Slice the lemons into smaller pieces – be careful not to squeeze the juice out of them.

3 Put half the lemons, half the raspberries and half the sugar into the food processor. Add a dash of sparkling water. Whizz until the lemons are mushy.

5 Repeat steps 3 and 4 with the rest of the lemons, raspberries and sugar.

4 Place the sieve over the jug. Carefully pour the mixture into the sieve, pushing it through with the spoon.

6 Add 750ml sparkling water and a handful of ice cubes to the jug. Keep cool in a flask.

BADGE LINK

Cook

PICNIC GEAR

☆ What else do you need for a perfect picnic? Something sweet to finish off the feast? Tangy jam tarts, yummy chocolate cupcakes or cool fresh strawberries?

☆ Remember a rug or plastic sheet to sit on. And don't forget plates and cups. Use plastic, not paper, so you can wash them up then use them again.

☆ What about a game or two? Turn the page for some great picnic games.

No one's quite sure where the word 'picnic' comes from. The original idea was that everyone should bring some food to share.

Picnic pastimes

'Is there a cricket bat and ball buried at the back of a cupboard? Or a Frisbee gathering dust under your bed? Shake off the cobwebs for some picnic fun and games!'

French cricket

YOU WILL NEED
- ☆ sports bat
- ☆ tennis ball

1 One person is the Batter. Everyone else stands in a large semicircle with the Batter in the centre. The Batter holds the bat like this.

2 Take turns to throw the ball at the Batter's legs. Aim below her knees and throw underarm.

3 The Batter must use the bat to stop the ball hitting her legs. She is not allowed to move her feet.

4 A player who hits the Batter's legs or catches the ball once it is hit becomes the next Batter.

Make it harder for an expert Batter. Pass the ball between players before throwing it to take the Batter by surprise!

Frisbee bowls

Before you recycle bottles or cans from your picnic, reuse them as skittles.

YOU WILL NEED
☆ a Frisbee
☆ empty plastic bottles or cans
☆ piece of string or some coats

1 Position the skittles in a triangle like this.

2 Mark a starting line 20 steps from the skittles.

3 Take turns to throw the Frisbee at the skittles from behind the starting line.

For each skittle you knock over, you get one point. If you knock them all over with one throw, you get ten points.

Silly statues

You don't need anything for this game.

1 One player is It.

2 The other players pretend to be statues. You must be completely still and keep a straight face.

3 The player who is It has to make the statues smile or laugh by staring, making funny faces or doing a silly dance. No tickling though!

4 Any statue who laughs is out. The statue who lasts the longest becomes the next It.

Krystle's puzzling pastimes
Island games

BADGE LINK
Sports
World issues

'The International Island Games bring sportsmen and sportswomen together from small islands around the world. The 2011 games are in the Isle of Wight.'

IN THE BASKET

Grace and Gwen Dubois are identical twin sisters and basketball stars. Can you tell which girls are Grace and Gwen?

ALL IN A KNOT

These three gymnasts have got their ribbons all in a knot. Follow the ribbons to find out who won which prize.

Illustrated by Andi Good

ON THE BALL

Oh dear! One of the players in the golf tournament has lost her ball. Can you find it for her?

A-MAZING TRAINING

Lotty Legstrong has got lost while training for the cycling competition. Can you help her get back to the stadium?

START

FINISH

NET DIFFERENCE

Can you spot ten differences between the pictures of this exciting volleyball game?

MAKE A SPLASH

Find the missing jigsaw piece to find out who won the swimming race.

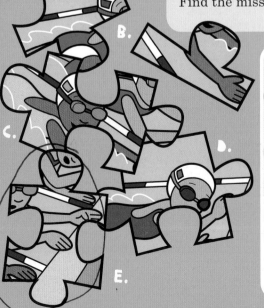

A.

B.

C.

D.

E.

73

Sally's best books
Top ten reads

'There are so many brilliant books, so how do you choose which ones to read? These are my top ten favourites. Best read them before you reach ten!'

BADGE LINK
Booklover
Hobbies

Good old fun

THE FAMILY FROM ONE END STREET by Eve Garnett

There are seven children in the Ruggles family. They don't have lots of money but they have plenty of lovely adventures and lots of fun. If you enjoy this, you may also enjoy *My Naughty Little Sister* by Dorothy Edwards.

THE BORROWERS by Mary Norton

The Clock family are very, very small and live under the floorboards of a country house! They 'borrow' and recycle household objects and get into all kinds of funny scrapes.

Fantasy

THE FARAWAY TREE COLLECTION by Enid Blyton

When Jo, Bessie and Fanny move to a new home they discover an Enchanted Wood and the Faraway Tree. So begins lots of magical adventures with the children's new friends. If you enjoy this, why not read *Haroun and the Sea of Stories* by Salman Rushdie?

Are you a serious Harry Potter fan and don't know what to read now? Why not try Children of the Red King series by Jenny Nimmo?

Adventure

KENSUKE'S KINGDOM by Michael Morpurgo

When Michael falls overboard from his parents' yacht and is washed up on an island he must fend for himself. He soon realises he is not alone… If this is your style of book, why not read *The Adventures of Tom Sawyer* by Mark Twain?

TOM'S MIDNIGHT GARDEN by Philippa Pearce

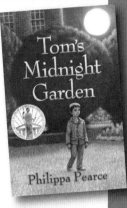

Tom is bored staying at his aunt's house, until one night he hears the old grandfather clock strike 13! He discovers a magical garden that everyone says doesn't exist.

DANNY THE CHAMPION OF THE WORLD by Roald Dahl

Think you know everything about the grown-ups you live with? Danny does, until he discovers his dad's incredible secret. Other great reads like this are *The Railway Children* by E Nesbit and *Moonfleet* by JM Falkner.

Animals

CHARLOTTE'S WEB by EB White

Fern loves her sweet little Wilbur, but Wilbur will soon have to leave with the other pigs. Can Charlotte, the beautiful and clever spider, save him? Try reading *The Sheep-Pig* by Dick King-Smith if you enjoy this story.

BLACK BEAUTY by Anna Sewell

Follow the eventful life of Black Beauty, a handsome stallion, who has many different owners, some kind and some cruel. Black Beauty keeps his unique spirit through it all. Other great horsey stories are in the Pony Club Secrets series by Stacy Gregg.

Growing up

OTHERWISE KNOWN AS SHEILA THE GREAT by Judy Blume

Sheila hates swimming and dogs and ghosts and thunderstorms – or does she? When summer comes, Sheila has to prove she's really Sheila the Great. Another good read about growing up is *Sleepovers* by Jacqueline Wilson.

SHRINKING VIOLET by Jean Ure

Violet's twin sister, Lily, is noisy, has a million friends and is always at a party. Violet is quieter and finds herself a penfriend instead. When Violet tells a few little fibs to keep her new friend interested she never thinks they will actually meet…

75

Cover of *Tom's Midnight Garden* by Philippa Pearce (OUP, 2008), reproduced by permission of Oxford University Press. Cover from *Kensuke's Kingdom* and The Faraway Tree collection, all published by Egmont UK Ltd London and used with permission. Covers from *The Family from One End Street*, *The Borrowers*, *Danny the Champion of the World*, *Charlotte's Web* and *Black Beauty* all reproduced by kind permission of Puffin Books. Cover from *Shrinking Violet* © 2002 Jean Ure. *Otherwise Known as Sheila the Great* by Judy Blume © published by Macmillan Children's Books.

Answers

Check out how well you did with all the fab Brownie Annual puzzles.

PAGE 15 - CROSS NUMBERS

Across:		Down:	
1. 144	5. 16	1. 10	7. 85
2. 13	6. 20	2. 1910	8. 75
3. 99	7. 80	4. 3000	
4. 36	9. 500	6. 24	
	10.35		

PAGE 15 - ANCIENT NUMBERS

II + III = V (2 + 3 = 5)
XXV + V = XXX (25 + 5 = 30)
VI – I = V (6 – 1 = 5)
L – VII = XLIII (50 – 7 = 43)
XI + IV = XV (11 + 4 = 15)
And, finally, what's MMXI? 2011

PAGE 52 - CREEPY-CRAWLY CROSSWORD

Across:	Down:
1. Cocoon	1. Centipede
4. Ant	2. Nit
7. Bee	3. Fleas
8. Poisonous	5. Cricket
9. Wasp	6. Glowworm
10. Moth	

PAGE 53 - BUTTERFLY HUNT

A	B	B	S	B	L	U	E	O	H	H
R	R	C	N	C	A	I	S	R	A	A
I	O	E	O	O	O	A	U	A	C	I
N	W	R	U	M	D	P	L	N	K	R
G	N	H	T	M	O	E	P	G	B	S
L	B	R	I	A	P	A	H	E	E	T
E	N	R	E	T	A	C	U	T	R	R
T	A	U	N	S	E	O	R	I	R	E
L	M	O	N	A	R	C	H	P	Y	A
K	H	P	B	U	C	K	E	Y	E	K

PAGES 30-31 - BIG BROWNIE SLEEPOVER

76

PAGE 53 - MIXED UP MINI-BEASTS

1. Fly 2. Worm 3. Spider 4. Beetle 5. Ladybird

PAGE 53 - WORM'S EYE VIEW

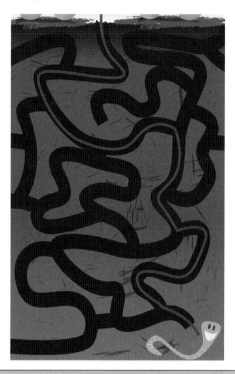

PAGE 66 - CRACK THE CODE

Dear Sally,
You're invited to visit 15th Powell Guides next Wednesday from 19.30 to 21.00 hours. So far this term, we've been getting all creative doing our Artists badge, and learning about the environment with Go For It! GRRReen. We're looking forward to our annual Patrol cooking competition at the end of term, and are busy planning what we're going to get up to on our summer camp. We can't wait to meet you!
From,
Puffin Patrol

PAGE 67 - MEET THE PUFFINS

L-R: Aicha, Emily, Jo, Becky, Hannah.

PAGE 67 - GUIDE CAMP

There are 8 creatures with Sally making her Promise.

PAGE 72 - IN THE BASKET

2 and 8 are the identical twins

PAGE 72 - ALL IN A KNOT

1st Bethany, 2nd Cate, 3rd Angel

PAGE 73 - ON THE BALL

PAGE 73 - NET DIFFERENCE

PAGE 73 - A-MAZING TRAINING

PAGE 73 - MAKE A SPLASH

The correct piece is E.